I0464660

From Zero To $12 Million To Bust!

INC 5000 CEO REVEALS HOW TO AVOID THESE
9 HIDDEN TRAPS THAT CAN DESTROY YOUR
BUSINESS

Amit Mehta

Copyright © 2015 by Amit Mehta.

All rights reserved. No part of this publication may be reproduced, distributed or transmitted in any form or by any means, including photocopying, recording, or other electronic or mechanical methods, without the prior written permission of the publisher, except in the case of brief quotations embodied in critical reviews and certain other noncommercial uses permitted by copyright law. For permission requests, write to the publisher, addressed "Attention: Permissions Coordinator," at the address below.

To my wife, Shilpi Mehta, who stood by my side and supported me through all my business ventures.

Contents

Forward

Amit is a young entrepreneur who thought he had the world at his fingertips.

He had struggled a bit in the beginning building his company, as all startup executives should. Boost Software was rocking along. It had grown from zero to $11.5 million. In sales in just over a year. Good enough to earn a high ranking in the Inc. 5000. He had a business partner and a team of developers. He did so many things right, after all cash was streaming in.

Unfortunately, as I have come to realize, Boost Software was too successful in that first year. If only Amit and his team had experienced even a few of the obstacles they encountered in their second full year of operation, the company still might be on its upward path. Quick wealth would not have conquered common sense. The need to covet cash would have been more important and the speed of growth would have been tempered with the need to step back and take a look at the big picture.

In a very relaxed prose, Amit tells his story about how his company began, conquered the market and subsequently fell to forces he never thought he would ever encounter. Through his journey, Amit learned many valuable lessons about business, people, markets and the realities of growing a successful enterprise. He uses this book to help readers recognize and hopefully avoid the same mistakes he has made.

The accompanying videos are used to reinforce and further clarify some of the topics covered in the book.

Everyone has their unique style and character. Amit is a very friendly professional that is always optimistic which occasionally gets him in trouble, but in the end his determination and beliefs will take him far in business. He is already planning his comeback. I am looking forward to see what he does next.

John Ireland, Guilford, CT

Risk Hacking

A Rude Awaking

Naïve.

That's the best way to describe myself back in early 2010 when my new business partner and I decide to start a software company over a Skype conversation.

I had NO idea what I was signing up for – it was a LOT more than I bargained for! In my last business, I had been a marketing "guru," selling information products. Before that, I had made money in affiliate marketing for a couple years.

I'd previously been a small business person. I didn't really have a team or any real employees. I had no prior experience in scaling up an equity business. My previous businesses had all been cash businesses. So I honestly didn't *really* understand what I was doing when I started Boost Software.

They say that making mistakes is the best way to learn.

I'd have to agree. Building Boost was the greatest learning experience of my life.

However, there's an easier, less painful way: *Learning from the mistakes of others.* And that's what this book is about. Specifically learning from *my* mistakes. We did a lot of things right as well, that helped us hit Inc 5000. I'll talk about that too.☺

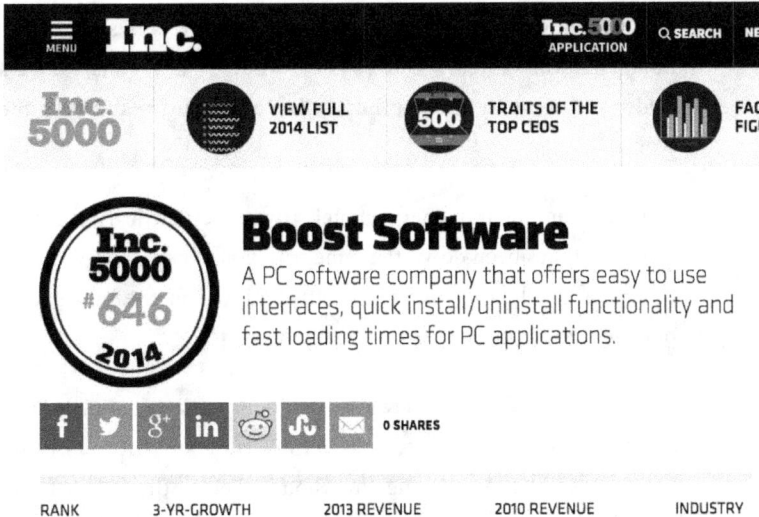

RANK	3-YR-GROWTH	2013 REVENUE	2010 REVENUE	INDUSTRY
646	**711%**	**$11.6 M**	**$1.4 M**	**Software**

Before I go on, I need to tell you that this book is NOT for everyone.

This book is NOT for you if:

1. If you're looking for business theory, with carefully researched and referenced citations from peer-reviewed articles.

2. If you're bored and are looking for shits and giggles.

3. If you have the ego the size of the Hindenburg (I did), and you think you already know everything you need to know about your business.

4. If you're looking to get rich quick.

If any of the above 4 points describes you, then this book is not for you, put it down and walk away.

However, this is the exact book for you if:

1. You're looking to start a business or already have a business that's doing millions a year. You consider yourself a visionary and a leader and want to make an impact in your industry and even the world!

2. You are humble and smart enough to realize that learning from someone that's been down the same path you're going on (or about to go on), will save you from getting kicked in the gut, sucker punched, and knocked down repeatedly.

3. You understand that there's tremendous risk in launching a business, and most of those risks are *hidden*. You want to discover how to defuse these ticking time bombs before they blow up in your face.

Risk Hacking

Speaking of hidden risks, I want to introduce you to a concept called risk hacking.

Ok, I admit the term "hacking" and "hacks" is so overused, but let's just go with it anyway because it really illuminates what I'm trying to get across.

I'm going to show you how to risk hack your business, whether you're just starting out or have a 5 million dollar business. As you're sitting down and reading this book, you'll find these lessons *invaluable*.

Before I talk about risk hacking, let's talk about growth hacking, a term that's bandied about a lot.

There's a lot of talk about "growth hacking" and how to "growth hack" your business. Growth hacks are basically strategies and tactics that you can use to supercharge your sales, marketing, and strategy to explode your sales.

5

All so you can punch the greed glands of a bigger company and sell your startup for a huge mountain of cash.

That all sounds good, however, why do so few startups, even the ones that have fast growth initially, actually accomplish the coveted "take the money and run" exit?

Because they likely triggered one (or more) of these 9 hidden traps, hidden risks, mistakes, whatever you want to call them that I talk about in this book.

I made mistakes in 2010, 2011, and 2012. I made mistakes in 2013. All these mistakes came back to haunt me in 2014.

That's right. It took years before the business felt the full brunt of all the disastrous decisions I had made.

Why?

Because it can take one, two, or even three years before your business feels the full effect of many of the mistakes you may be making right now – you'll understand why as you read the book.

It's like a ticking time bomb; these mistakes can come back and blow up a huge chunk of your business, causing *irreparable* damage.

If this happens to your business, and it's limping along on crutches, it's only a matter of time before your competitors put your business out of its misery. As you read this book, chapter to chapter, I'll show you how to avoid this fate.

I know. I still haven't actually defined what risk hacking is?!?

Risk hacking is identifying and neutralizing the most common hidden risks that your business will face. Many of these hidden risks can do irreparable damage, as they did to Boost.

What was really frustrating was that by 2014, I knew I had made all of these mistakes. I knew the company was in a horrible position, but it was at a point of no return. I was at a point where I couldn't undo the mistakes.

> Risk hacking will not only help prevent your business from going down, but it will also help grow your business *sustainably and profitably* and have investors (and buyers) licking their chops for a piece of the action.

The damage was already done, and I was trying to dig myself out of the hole. It was more like a black hole.

However, it's not too late to reverse and limit the damage of bad decisions, *if you act fast.*

In the next 9 chapters, I'm going to walk you through the EXACT critical missteps that wrecked an 8-figure company and how you can prevent them from destroying your business.

Some Embarrassing and Damaging Admissions

I'm going to reveal a lot about myself and my business in this book. Stuff that most people would never talk publicly about. Some of it is going to seriously piss some people off.

Why am I doing this? Because I feel I need to be as open and honest as possible to reveal all the hidden risks I stumbled upon. There's an underlying theme to these risk that I'm going to dig up.

It has to do with mindset, thought process, and strategy. Yeah, that includes some tear-jerking emotional stuff as well. Being successful in business is 2% mechanics and 98% thought process. Someone who has their headspace right while working 40 hours a week will CRUSH someone who doesn't, even though they are working 80 hours a week. Every time.

In the spirit of openness and honesty, I'm going to divulge some very embarrassing and damaging admissions:

1. I have no formal training in business, marketing or finance. My degree is in Physics, as far as away from business as you can get!

2. I failed reading in the 1st grade. In fact, they put me in a remedial class with all the "special" kids. That did wonders for my self-esteem! I later discovered I was dyslexic.

3. Boost was very publicly sued by the FTC. Claiming our PC optimizer was bogus and our marketing was misleading.

Before you run screaming, "OMG this guy is a scammer!" Let me give you the punchline. We won against the FTC in court, proving our product is REAL and our marketing is not deception. In fact, we had an expert witness, who wrote 17 books on Windows®, testify to prove our case.

What a shocker, the government gets things wrong sometimes!

Getting sued by the government is something I would not wish on my worst enemy. It's the 7th level of business hell. Your business is shut down. Your brand is destroyed overnight; all your vendors and channels partners turn against you. All while drowning in 6-figure legal fees.

I still remember the day like it was yesterday. I saw a guy walking up my lawn, holding a stack of files probably about two-feet high. He was a constable.

He knocked on my door, and he asked me, "*Hey, is this Amit Mehta?*" I said, "*Yes.*" He handed me the stack of papers. And I went to my desk in the other room. I put the stack of paper on my desk. All I saw was FTC something, something, something suing my company, and my jaw hit the floor.

I immediately sat down. I chatted to my business partner. I said, *"It's over. We're done."* We had just gotten served a civil lawsuit by the Federal Trade Commission. It was November 12, 2014. I didn't know how to react. I was in complete shock. I couldn't believe it.

Ten days later, we fought them in court. I worked my butt off, and assembled a legal team. Cost us around $150,000. Fought it in court. We won. We proved we were legit.

We earned the right to turn our business back on without restriction.

This was an amazing victory because beating the government in court is near impossible.

I was celebrating and my team was celebrating, when only days later we came to realize we weren't going back to business. Certainly not in the way we were doing business in November when we were generating $30,000 a day in revenue with a run rate of $10 million for the year 2014.

We were going out of business. The truth of the matter hit me in the head like a pile of bricks.

I contacted our channel partners and our vendors and said, *"Hey, we won against the FTC. We can turn our business back on. Hooray! Let's get our traffic turned back on."*

They said, *"Great, Amit. We need the payment for your last invoice and then we'll be happy to turn your traffic back on so you can start generating sales again."*

I said, *"There's no way we can pay the last invoice."* Because

- Fighting the FTC cost us $150,000 in legal fees.

- The FTC shut down our business for 3 weeks

- The FTC withheld all the commissions we made from our call center in the month of November.

Guess what? They didn't quite go for that. They said, *"You need to pay up first before we can turn your business back on,"* and that wasn't going to happen.

In total, the estimated damage was easily a million dollars, more if you include the brand damage. So there's no way we could pay our channel partners. I was hopping mad at first, but then I tried to see things from their perspective: **would you try to feed a fatally wounded animal?**

At this point, I had to make the heart-wrenching decision to lay off 20 employees in the month of December, right before Christmas. I had people breakdown crying on the phone – not fun. ☹

I thought back. I took some time to really think back over everything that had happened. How did I get to this point? I realized that the FTC was merely the straw that broke the camel's back. The company was in serious financial straits all through 2014.

We were running at break-even. We had taken out a considerable amount of debt from a local bank. We were paying it back, and paying back the debt was crushing us. On top of that, we had a couple of nasty surprises happen in 2014 that cost us hundreds of thousands of dollars.

All of this hit while our business was hanging on to the edge of a cliff, holding on with three fingers. The FTC took a butcher knife and chopped those 3 fingers off.

Why was our business in dire straits in 2014? It has everything to do with the 9 hidden traps you're about to discover as you read on.

In next chapter, I reveal a deadly trap you must avoid when you first launch your business.

CHAPTER 1

Your Foundation

The Foundation is the Most Important Part of a House

I still remember it like it was yesterday, I was a small child and my parents were having a custom home built. A big upgrade from the small home we were currently living in. In a nicer neighborhood too.

My parents had scrimped and saved for years to make the down payments for this house.

We drove by our new home every week to see how things were going. I remember they spent a VERY long time on the foundation. Weeks passed, even months, and it was all foundation, foundation, foundation.

Once the foundation was done, it was *amazing* how fast the rest of the house was built.

The foundation is the most important part of your home. If your foundation is not done right, it will cause serious problems and destroy the resale value of your home.

And it costs a fortune to fix a foundation.

So what does this have to do with your business?

Listen carefully...

As you read the rest of the chapter, you'll discover why decisions you make when you first launch your business, *your foundational decisions*, will determine whether you succeed or fail.

In this chapter, I will risk hack these foundational decisions:

1. Who you choose to partner up with

2. How much equity to dish out to your new business partners

As you'll see, setting up the relationship right with the right set of business partners is *absolutely critical*.

Sadly, this is one of the most common mistakes people make when starting their first business.

The Biggest Mistake I Made Early On

I approached a friend of mine who I'd worked with before. I knew he was a very smart guy, because he was making more money than me as an affiliate!

I asked him if he wanted to go into business with me. My plan was to build our own PC optimizer, and use our marketing expertise to sell it. We both had broken records selling PC optimizer products as affiliates, so we figured we could be more successful if we actually created our own.

Without a thought, I gave him 50% of the company.

Don't get me wrong. He was an AWESOME business partner. He was sharp as a whip, and always came up with amazing creative ideas. We worked very well together for years. And I could not have build built Boost without him.

However, it quickly became apparent that I would be *completely funding the entire venture,* because my business partner was *never* in a financial condition to put any money in the company.

I would end up bankrolling the company right up until the end. This is what I got me really rung out over. Carry the financial burden of the entire company on my shoulders was almost too much to bare. I'll get into how that played out in a later chapter. For now let's just say it became UGLY.

We did agree that I would get the first $200,000 in profits generated because I was bankrolling the company. Giving away 50% of your company for the promise of first dibs on the profits (if any) in the future is a BAD IDEA. Especially for a paltry $200k.

Think about it.

If the company had gone bust before it ever generated a profit, I would have been financially wiped out while my partner would have lost ZERO because he put in nothing.

We were not profitable until mid to late 2012, over 2 ½ years later. ☹

During that time, I took all the financial risk, even borrowed money from my family TWICE. And put myself and my wife under the soul-crushing burden of constant financial strain.

The company almost went bust 3 times during that period - more about that later.

I can't tell you how many nights I lost sleep. My wife had panic attacks in the middle of the night. Panic attacks. There were stretches of weeks where I had near panics attacks on a daily basis.

If I Had to Do It All Over Again...?

A lot of people asked, *"Amit, if you had a chance to do it all over again, how would you have structured the deal?"*

I would have done 80% - 20% equity split. **Not a percent more.**

Now am I being greedy here? Absolutely not.

If I'm bankrolling the entire venture then anyone I bring on should be lucky if I give them any equity, especially if they don't have any extraordinary skills above and beyond what I have.

The Exception

Now if I was partnering with someone who had built and sold 10 companies for 8-figures a pop or a programming wizard who had created a revolutionary software program, then that's different situation all together.

Why?

Because they're bringing something to the table that is extraordinary, and I'd be happy to bankroll the company and still hand them a big chunk of equity.

If you're giving away 50% of your equity to your business partner and they are not bringing anything extraordinary to the table, then *they better match every cent you put into the company.*

Don't get me wrong, my business partner was a brilliant guy, as I mentioned before. However, he basically had the same skill sets that I did.

To be fair, if the tables were turned, and he was funding the company, then it would not make sense for me to take more than 20% equity.

The Infamous Cash Call

Let's say, in the beginning, both you and your partner threw in $10k in to the business. Now you need to put another $10,000 apiece into the business 2 months later and your business partner can't come up with the goods, then guess what?

You invest the $20,000 in the company and you now own 75% (assuming your company has not risen in value).

Confused? Here's how the math for that breaks down.

	Business Launch Investment	Equity	Investment after 2 months	Total Invested	Final Equity Split
You	$10,000	50%	$20,000	$30,000	75%
Partner	$10,000	50%	$0	$10,000	25%

Total amount invested in the company is $40,000. You invested $30,000. Congratulations you now own 75% of the company, and that's the way it has to be.

Now you might get some pushback from your business partner, he might say, *"Wait, can't you just lend the money to the business? If you put in $20,000, I will lose half my shares!"*

If you hear that early on, then I would immediately call it off and dissolve the business. **Because you have a moocher on your hands who wants something for nothing.**

And if you agree to this ridiculous arrangement of ~~risking~~ loaning your money to the company, so your partner can hold onto his equity and voting rights, then it will come back and bite you in the ass so hard you'll wish you never started the company in the first place.

Get a backbone and stand up for what's rightfully yours.

Your business partner will come up with a million excuses why he doesn't have the money and how it's not fair. Don't fall for emotional blackmail.

There's one big reason why you can't give away half your equity to a business partner who can't pony up the cash: **commitment.**

The Business Partner Default

A partner who refuses to put money into the business is like someone buying a house zero down.

Why are banks so reluctant to give you a home mortgage without any down payment? Because they know, statistically, you are more likely to default if you didn't put any money down.

It's called "skin in the game."

If your business partner does not have any skin in the game, that's fine. He might contribute a lot to your team and a lot to your company. However, you can't give him 50 percent. You have to fight for every cent of equity you can.

You say, "Great. We're going to bring you on. We'll give you 20 percent, and you're going to do your part. Since I'm bankrolling this company, I will take the overwhelming majority of shares and voting rights."

If you give them half the company, and they haven't put any money in, guess what? Justas a homeowner who hasn't put any money towards their down payment is more likely to default, your business partner is also more likely to default, having put no money in.

And that's exactly what happened to me.

In 2014, my business partner defaulted, after years of working hard for the company. He all of a sudden mentally checked out of the business.

I was in complete SHOCK.

It's a crazy story.

I had taken a couple of my top managers to a program called "Key Executive Program," sponsored by EO Network.

There was a social event on the last night, where we were making mixed drinks. One of my employees got punch drunk.

They spilled the beans on everything my employees were saying behind my back.

All the stuff that they talked about amongst themselves, but didn't divulge to me.

Here's the shocker...

They flat-out told me that my business partner had completely checked out.

In fact, they told me my partner was only working 12 hours *a week*.

Furthermore, everyone in the company felt that my partner was hurting the company.

They pleaded with me, *"Amit, you have to do something about it because he's destroying the company."*

My jaw hit the floor.

Honestly, I knew that he had not been at 100 percent. However, I didn't know how serious it was. Maybe because he was my business partner, I was just blinded to the fact that he had dropped the ball.

He had *defaulted* on the company.

This was all a result of a decision I had made in 2010 of giving him 50% of the company. THAT mistake came back to haunt me years later.

Even earlier on, I realized that there were some issues with his commitment. He didn't want to fully participate in team meetings. He was reluctant want to travel. His commitment just was not to the level that my commitment was.

I had risked my savings, *my personal savings,* to build the company. My personal commitment was a lot higher **because I risked everything**. And I kept risking my own money all the way up to the end.

In my business partner's defense, he later disclosed to me later on that he had completely burned out. Given the condition of the company at the time and what we were dealing with, I couldn't blame him.

I was half burned out myself. I'll tell you more later.

Anyways, we had a situation where I had to do a cash call (where you ask all equity partners to put money in the company) in 2014. The company badly needed a cash infusion to stay afloat. I put in $130,000 into the company. My business partner put in nothing.

My partner wanted me to loan the money to the company so he could keep 50% of the company and keep his 50% voting rights. He was afraid I would fire him.

I was hopping mad. I threatened to let the company go bust if he didn't let me get my fair equity share for the money I was putting in. In tears, he caved.

I drained a big chunk of my personal savings to make payroll for the company in 2014.

On the upside, I secured majority voting rights in the company. Now, I had almost complete control of the company. I used this power to FORCE my business partner to invest in the company.

If he wasn't going to contribute anything to the company, then I would simply cut both of our salaries.

So we were, in effect, contributing half our salaries to the company to help it during tough financial times.

Sadly, handing out equity like candy is a very common mistake many new business owners make. A lot of times, people will give ½ their business away to someone who they could have hired for $3,000 - $5,000 a month. Someone with no exceptional skills to speak of.

Giving away ½ your company is like handing somebody a gold bar. They can run away with it. They can take it. They can bury it in the backyard. And *you'll never get it back.*

If your business takes off, your business partner can literally disappear or decide to work 12 hours a week and there's nothing you can do. You gave them 50% of the business; you can't even fire them without their approval!

Hedging Your Risk

It's even risky giving someone 10% of your company.

What if your business partner goes crazy after a year? What if he loses heart in the business? What if he mentally checks out? He's now a dead weight weighing your company down.

Yeah, you can fire him. But he still has equity in your company. You won't get that equity back unless you buy them out, and that will cost you an arm and a leg.

Is there a way around this? Not 100%, but there are ways to mitigate the risk to the company.

Instead of giving a partner 20% equity upfront, vest that equity over multiple years.

What does that mean?

It simply means you don't give your partner all the equity all at once; you just give them a small piece every year.

So, for example, a partner with 20% percent vested over 5 years would get 4% equity EACH year for five years. See the table below...

Years	1	2	3	4	5
Equity	4%	8%	12%	16%	20%

What's great about that strategy is that your partner is actually earning his equity. If your business partner disappears after a year, he doesn't walk away with a huge chunk of the company.

You've dramatically mitigating the risk to the company.

You can even have all partners vest their equity over time. Or do an earn in, where partners have to hit specific milestones to earn their equity. More about that in my video training.

The Buy/Sell

The other thing you want in place is a buy/sell agreement. A buy/sell agreement is for exactly the scenario where your partner goes cuckoo or he loses heart or he just disappears or something. With a buy/sell agreement in place, you can force your partner to sell his share.

Planning for "shit has hit the fan" contingencies will shield your business from an otherwise fatal death blow.

A buy/sell agreement also protects you if your partner dies, and the shares go to his spouse. The agreement will ensure that you have control of the company (especially important if you're 50/50), and allow you to buy out the shares from the spouse.

FREE BUSINESS GROWTH ACCELERATION VIDEOS

Want to discover more strategies on how to mitigate business risk *and* grow you're business faster than you ever imagined?

WARNING: This is like nothing you've seen before. These videos are a little weird.

After clicking the link below and opting in, you'll get immediate access to my series of Business Growth Acceleration videos.

http://profitswami.com/bookbonus

As you watch each video you'll discover new strategies, tactics, and tools that will allow you to smash through barriers holding your business back. Helping you achieve the success and recognition you deserve.

CHAPTER 2

Cash Versus Equity Business

As you're sitting back and reading through this chapter, you'll discover the crucial difference between equity versus cash, and why mixing the two can become a lethal cocktail.

Here's the bottom line...

You must understand the difference between building an equity business or a cash business because if you don't, you'll burn your business to the ground in a short-lived blaze of glory.

You may think your business is a cash business when it might, in fact, be an equity business. What is a cash business?

Cash Businesses Can ROCK

I was used to building cash businesses with *minimum* overhead – it was a pretty sweet deal while it lasted.

I'd make $50,000 a month in gross profits with $5,000 a month in overhead. I had a couple outsourcers, server cost, etc. **I had a well-oiled money machine, all I had to do was turn a few levers and polish a few rough edges every week and it would hum along spitting out huge amounts of cash.**

Now just to be clear I did NOT actually print money, because that's illegal. I sold affiliate and information products online! It was so easy that it felt like I was printing money, *legally!*

I had a truly kickass cash-based business. Not a retail business where you slave away for 12 hours a day to make $5,000 a month net. Or a consulting business where you traded hours for dollars. I had a Timothy Ferris 4-hour work-week type business, and I loved it!

Whatever profit I had left at the end of the month was *my income.* I put away a portion for quarterly taxes, a little bit for savings, a little bit for donations, and the rest would just collect in my bank account. At any given time, I had over $100,000 in my personal checking account.

Yes, all else being equal, money does bring happiness. Having a $100,000+ in your checking account is a damn good feeling. ☺

Sorry to digress, my point is, cash businesses ROCK if you build them correctly. **Did my business have any resell value? Very little. However, I didn't care because I was banking so much cash on a monthly basis that it didn't matter.**

Equity Businesses are a Long Term Play

Now Boost, the company that I was building, was an equity business. We were developing a line of software. Before we were forced to slam the doors shut, we had 20 full-time employees. Our payroll was $150,000 a MONTH between our employees, contractors and outsourcers. Boost was burning more cash on payroll in the month than I spent per year on overhead for my previous businesses.

We had a full staff of around 30 between our contractors, employees, and everyone else. I never quite understood the stress of "making payroll" until now. A lot of people were depending on me, and I couldn't let them down!

An equity business is a long-term play. The goal is to build up the value of the company and sell it down the road for a lifetime of riches, fame, fortune, and glory!

You are trading a huge pot of gold at the end of the rainbow far away in exchange living frugally, on a modest income, and investing the rest right back into your business.

That's the price you must pay. If you try to have your cake and eat it, you're treading on thin ice.

Now you may be asking, *"What exactly do you mean by building up the value of the company?"*

I delve more into that in my free video series. In short, building value of an equity business is about:

1. Building a winning team
2. Building systems to maintain, grow, and improve business
3. Creating brand and mindspace for your company, products, and services
4. Building out your product/service line
5. Developing multiple strong, profitable, and sustainable sales channels and partnerships
6. Etc...

Growth SUCKS UP cash. And if you ain't got any, you're in trouble!

The list goes on, but you get the idea. *All of these items suck up a lot of resources and gobble up huge stacks of cash to develop.*

The Death Trap of Success

In 2013, Boost sales and profits went through the roof. We had enough money in the bank to swim in. Nearly $1million in cold hard cash.

Our cash flow was INSANE.

I had worked hard to setup to setup 15-30 day net terms with all our channel partners, on top of having $500,000 credit line on my American Express Black card.

<u>Our cash conversion cycle was NEGATIVE</u>. That is, for every advertising dollar we spend today, we had already made money on it 7-10 days prior.

This is where things got REALLY dangerous. Yeah, that's right, the greatest danger is when money is pouring in and you're celebrating how brilliant you are.

WHY?

Because that's when you:

1. Develop a massive ego (the size of the Hindenburg!) and think you have it all figured out. Hubris – the classic character flaw that lead to the downfall of almost every Greek hero!
2. Think the gravy train will last forever, and that things will just get better and better, and better!
3. Lose your focus and sense of urgency, the very things that made you successful in the first place.

Confusing Equity Versus Cash

Guess what I did when I saw the huge mountain of cash sitting in the Boost bank account?

I decided to take large distributions out of the company. I bought a house, invested a bunch of it, and put a lot of money into my house.

Now, since I had a business partner that was 50/50, I had to match my distributions with him, **which meant taking DOUBLE the money out of the business!**

Equal number of bars of gold for each of us! Think of the movie "Italian Job."

I treated Boost like a cash business. UGHH.

We did almost three million dollars EBITDA that year. Both my business partner and I took out close to a million a piece.

Everything was going great until....

To Be Continued in Chapter 3!

FREE BONUS VIDEOS

Want to discover breakthrough strategies on how to mitigate business risk *and* grow you're business faster than you ever imagined?

WARNING: This is like nothing you've seen before. These videos are a little weird.

After clicking the link below and opting in, you'll get immediate access to my series of Business Growth Acceleration videos.

http://profitswami.com/bookbonus

As you watch each video you'll discover unorthodox cutting-edge strategies, tactics, and tools that will allow you to smash through barriers holding your business back. Helping you achieve the success and recognition you deserve.

CHAPTER 3

Cash, Taxes, and Debt

The Death Spiral

As you're reading this chapter, you'll discover how one bad mistake can create a domino effect and topple an 8-figure business, and hopefully, you will take to heart the strategies outlined on how your business can avoid this tragic fate.

Everything was going great for Boost until sales plunged at the end of 2013. **Our #1 sources of sales had completely dried up. Our oasis of profits had transformed into Death Valley.**

Now, that wouldn't have been a problem if we had a cash business with very little overhead costs

However, we had a huge payroll, and other expenses that go along with a business of our scale. We ended up in a dire situation where we had to dip into our savings to make payroll and cover operating expense.

It got so UGLY we had to borrow money to pay our taxes.

Attempting to borrow money when your company is cash strapped is not a fun situation. On top of that fact, we had less than 3 years of business history, and *banks hate that.*

To make matters even worse, most banks looked at us and said, "*Well, you basically sucked the company dry. You took out $2million in distributions. We're not loaning you a single cent.*" Can you blame them?

We did, unbelievably, manage to secure bank funding, but at a heavy price.

The death spiral had begun.

Living Frugally

If you want to build an equity business, you must take a *minimum salary* out. A minimum salary should be just enough to cover your living expenses.

You want to leave enough money in the company to build a war chest.

Why?

Because there are several frightening truths, you will face as you build your business.

For starters, no matter how smart you think you are, you will have downturns. It will not always be a walk in the park. That's just the process of building an equity business. There will inevitably be ups and downs. You need a big cash cushion to break your fall when you drop off the edge of a cliff, or you'll face a bloody demise.

So hold off on buying that sports car or buying that McMansion. It's a mistake that you may never be able to undo.

Taking out two million dollars in cash from my business as distributions was a tragic mistake that I could not undo.

And it still haunts me.

This one mistake would have disastrous consequences. It would create a domino effect that would bring Boost to the chopping block. Begging for a quick death.

I'll get into the gory details later. First, I want to show you how you can prevent this fate.

How to Build an Impregnable Ship

Cherish the times when you have strong growth. When your company has a dump truck full of cash dropped into its bank account every month.

You want to bank as much cash as possible, preferably at least two to six months' worth of operating expenses or two months' worth of advertising expenses (if your company spends a lot on advertising). Save whichever amount is larger.

We spent up to $20,000-plus a day on advertising. If Boost had done the right thing and had a $1.2 million *after-tax* cash cushion (2 months of advertising), we'd likely be operating at full force today.

$1.2 million in the bank would have provided us with solid protection against our major sales channels suddenly plunging from massive profitability to zero in late 2013. We could have rebounded without too much sweat and tears.

Think of your company as a ship. The more cash you have, the stronger, more stable, and unsinkable your ship is.

Cash will get your company through those rough storms. And help it survive torpedoes from competitors.

Why the ship analogy?

In the old days, the idea of a corporation was originally created to mitigate risk when shipping goods across seas. If you were selling widgets to a vendor on the other side of the ocean, you were taking on a huge risk, because if your ship sunk, you would be personally liable for the losses, one bad storm could bankrupt you!

So the idea of a corporation was invented to protect personal assets against business risk. With a corporation in place, you risked only what you put on the ship and nothing more.

So you've got to think of your company as a ship. Your ability to survive rough waters and deadly storms is directly proportional to how much cash you have on hand. Once you run out of cash, your company will sink to the bottom very quickly.

Death and Taxes

Taxes are directly connected with cash. It's something you can easily overlook. Especially if you have a really good year! Tax time can be a very rude awakening if you're not prepared.

Boost got slapped with massive tax bill in 2014, after a killer 2013. Only problem was that we had drained our savings to cover operating expenses, on top of sucking the company dry with our distributions.

We had $400,000 in the bank and were staring at a $1.2million tax bill. ☹

It doesn't help that the government really punishes you when your company finally attains success. In Massachusetts, they slap you with a sting tax if you make over $6 million in revenue.

It's the government's way of thanking you.

Thank you for helping the economy. Thank you for hiring all those people. We're going to hit you with a 3 percent sting tax for all your success.

Tax Planning

We had talked to our accountant and our CFO about tax planning.

I should have fired him over this.

He said, *"Oh, don't worry about it. Just keep the money in the bank. Just pay it at the end of the year."*

I asked, *"Hey, should I have money withheld from my paycheck?"* He said, *"Oh, just take a minimum salary and take the rest in distributions."* So, naïvely, we did that. We stuck our head in the sand assuming we'd make enough through the business to cover our taxes next year.

We ended up borrowing $600,000 from a local bank. Because of our financial position we got raped on the payment terms. The bank demanded a 10-month repayment schedule at $60,000 a month!

We had to pay back $60,000 a month on top of just being barely profitable.

Boost was as fragile as a house of cards, all because we failed to make quarterly tax payments the year before.

Now, a lot of people might ask, *"If you had taken that money out to pay taxes, you couldn't have made payroll."* No, actually, if we had made quarterly payments in 2013, we would have made different decisions as the company progressed.

Here's what we would have done differently if we had made our quarterly tax payments:

1. I would have taken smaller distributions.

2. I would have been less aggressive on hiring and racking up overhead costs.

3. I would have had a greater sense of urgency and focus on building the business.

Confused?

Making $300,000 tax payments every 3 months would have given me a lot of perspective on the real financial situation of the company. *And not the way things appeared pre-tax.*

This is a point I'm going to hammer on repeatedly. **It is absolutely CRITICAL that you have an accurate pulse of the financial health of your company at ALL times.**

I'm talking about more than just your monthly P&L statement your bookkeeper sends you.

You need to have a solid grasp of your cash position, monthly cashflow, KPIs (key performance indicators). How is your company is performing on a weekly, even daily, basis? If you don't know, you're flying blind.

When I finally got this concept, I would watch money going in and out of the company like a crack addict.

The more accurate and current picture of the financial condition of your company, the better decisions you will make. It's not enough to depend on a CFO. You are the CEO. You MUST understand how to:

✓ Read a cashflow statement

✓ Review a balance sheet

✓   Understand your P&L

✓   Know which KPIs to track and how often to track them

Also, constantly ask these questions:

✓   How much cash do we have in the bank?

✓   What does my cashflow look like?

✓   How much do we have to pay in taxes? How much cash does that leave in the bank?

✓   What's my projected cash flow for the next quarter?

These questions will help you make better decisions. It's foolish to riskhack your business based on financials that paint an inaccurate, rosy picture.

And don't be scared if your business is in bad financial shape.

After taking a hard look at your true financial situation, you might think, *"Maybe we shouldn't do that huge, risky project. Let's stick with our core strengths and continue to solidify and grow our current standing in the market."*

> Facts are friendly. The sooner you face the facts, the sooner you can dig your company out of the hole - before it's too late.

Don't Touch or See that Cash Cushion!

Remember earlier how I talked about why it's critical to keep 2-6 months of operating expenses in the bank as a disaster/rainy day fund?

Well, I want to elaborate on that: 2-6 months of operating expenses are *on top of your quarterly tax savings.*

Let me use Boost as an example. Boost should have saved $300,000 a quarter for taxes, that's 1.2 million a year and 6 months of operating expenses on TOP of that. That comes to an additional $1.2million as a cash cushion.

That comes to $2.4million set aside for taxes and the company's cash cushion. Now Boost did $3million EBIDTA in 2013. That would have left $600,000 at the beginning of 2014 with taxes fully paid.

In reality, there would have been $1.2millon + $600,000 = $1.8 million in the bank, but I'm not counting the $1.2million.

Why?

Because that's our emergency fund. I can NOT look at that when making executive decisions. I would have put that money in a separate bank account and ignored it.

The $1.2million is a catastrophe fund, an all cash insurance policy. *Not to be touched unless the company runs dries.* As the company increases its operating expenses, I would add more money to this catastrophe fund.

You'll make different decisions if you look at your company as having *only* $600,000 in the bank, versus having $1.8million in the bank.

Don't you think?

If you already follow a cash strategy like the one I've outlined above. Congrats!

You still have lots of money to fuel your business. You'll likely never be in a position where you have to borrow money if you're sales suddenly dip.

You won't have to crawl on your hands and knees and beg a bank for money. Only to get flogged with a soul-sucking repayment schedule. And *that's if they agree to loan you any money.*

And it will put your company in an excellent position to qualify for a business line of credit.

Why should you get a line of credit if your business already has 2 months or more of operating expenses in the bank?

Because it will give you an *extra layer of protection* in the event that your business gets hit by a black swan calamity.

There's a lot of black swans that can sneak up and cripple your business:

➢ Your business gets sued.

➢ Your top sales channel suddenly stops producing. Your top sales person leaves. Or you lose a huge client out of the blue.

➢ Your business partner leaves or mentally checks out.

➢ New government regulations make your business model obsolete.

I could go on, but you get the idea!

TIP

A business line of credit is a form of debt I recommend every business get as soon as they qualify. And I even recommend you use it. Put a little bit on it and quickly pay it off in 2 to 3 months. The bank LOVES this. This strategy will help you build your credit history.

Banks don't get super excited if you take out a $100,000 line of credit and never use it. They don't make any money. Put $20,000 on there and pay it off every 3 months. Keep repeating the process. Then go back to the bank after a year and ask for a $200,000 line of credit.

Turning Debt into Profits

Debt can be a ticking time bomb that can destroy your business if abused and not handled *properly*. It's crucial you know when to take debt and when NOT to take debt.

Debt is leverage. There's raw power in leverage. By taking out debt, you are leveraging other people's money to accelerate the growth of your business. Funding growth is *the reason to take debt* on.

For example, let's say it cost you $500 to acquire a customer. If you borrow $500,000, that will allow you to accelerate the growth of your business, by allowing you to quickly acquire 1000 customers. *This could be enough to catapult your business light years ahead of your competitors.*

Especially if you have a business where you're billing customers on a monthly basis. Let's run through the numbers to give you a concrete example:

- It costs you $500 to acquire a customer – your CAC
- Each customer pays you $300/month
- The customer lifetime value (CLV) is $5,000
- $500,000 loan or line of credit allows you to quickly snatch up 1000 customers
- These 1000 new customers are now paying you 1000 x $300 = $300,000 PER MONTH
- Let's assume your cashflow on each customer is $200 (just an example!). $100 per customer is going towards payroll, overhead, etc.
- With a 1000 new customers, you're making $200k a month cashflow.
- It will take you 2.5 months to pay back the $500,000 loan. That's your cash on cash return.

Does that make sense? You've borrowed $500,000 to generate a $2.4mm a year in gross profits! I'll take those numbers all day long.

Now if you're smart and do things properly, you can reinvest that $2.4mm- $500k loan repayment = $1.9mm back into acquiring more customers, to grow your sales and profits even MORE.

In this circumstance, it makes a lot of sense to borrow money because it represents transactional value. You're borrowing and spending money today, which will fill your coffers with a mountain of cash down the road. Borrow and spend X today to make back 10X over time.

Now taking out a bank loan or a line of credit is not the only way to borrow money. It's tough to get a bank to loan you money in the beginning. Banks typically want to see 3 years of solid business history before their willing to pull out their checkbook for you.

Instead of loans, Boost used credit cards to fuel its growth. I had a $500,000 credit line on my American Express Black card. I would rack up $100,000+ a month of spend on my card and then pay it off 30 days later.

I also negotiated 15 to 30-day net terms with our channel partners. Boost ended up having a NEGATIVE cash conversion cycle. That is for every dollar we spend today, we had already generated a profit on it 7 to 14 days ago! Why? Because we could float our advertising spend for 30-45 days between my Black card and favorable net terms. We only paid adverting bill after we had our money in the bank. BOOYA. ☺

How to Negotiate Kickass Net Terms

Imagine if your business had an *unlimited sales and marketing budget* that allows you to explode your customer base and dominate your space.

I just talked about how Boost had a negative cash conversion cycle – allowing us to bank our profits before we paid a single cent on advertising. **This allowed us to aggressively ramp up our sales, spending**

$600,000-$800,000 a month on advertising and FLOAT that money for up to 30 days while sales poured into our bank account.

Locking in favorable net terms like these is both a science and an art. However, *if done right, you* can finally stop biting your nails. You can stop worrying about cashflow, and focus on the fun stuff: growth.

Here're a few strategies for securing favorable net terms:

- ✓ Contact the right person at the accounting department and say, *"Hey, we've been working with you for two months, I've spent $500,000. We've made all our payments in advance. Give us some net terms here. Give us 7-day net terms."*
- ✓ Once you secure 7-day net terms, keep paying them fast, well before the 7 days is up. Then after 2 months, come back and ask for 10-day net terms. Repeat this process every 2 months. Be assertive.
- ✓ Build a relationship with the accounting rep. Add them as a Facebook friend. Ask about their family. Send them a thank you card. Show your genuine appreciation.

Remember: Keep pushing for better and better terms. Rush your payments to them in advance. Show them that you're good for the money. This step is critical to improving your net terms.

Once you achieve a negative cash conversion cycle, *your cash flow will be even better than your profitability.* Because you'll have the money in the bank before your invoice comes due. *That's an enviable position to be in, for any business.*

Ways to Raise Money

There are a lot of other ways to raise money other than credit cards, bank loans, and net terms with your vendors and channel partners.

- ✓ **VC or angel investor**. This makes the most sense if you're in the startup phase.
- ✓ **Crowdsourcing** through sites like kickstarter.com
- ✓ **Debt-to-Equity instrument.** Where the money you borrow gets converted into equity in your company if you don't pay it back.
- ✓ **Cash call.** Ask everyone who has an equity stake to put cash into the company.

I'll get into the details of these strategies later. Check out my free bonus videos (link at the end of this chapter).

When NOT to take Debt

You NEVER EVER want to take debt if the company is limping along like a fatally wounded animal. Even if your company will likely go bankrupt without taking the debt.

Why would I say that? Because I've seen the devastation caused by taking debt you can't pay back.

Few points to keep in mind:

1. If your company is in financial straits, a bank will likely ONLY agree to loan you money if you personally guarantee it. That means if the company can't pay it back, YOU are personally on the hook.
2. You'll get LOUSY repayment terms.
3. Repaying the debt will suck the life out of you and your business

Boost took out $600,000 of *personally guaranteed* debt, with a 10-month repayment schedule. Yes, $60,000 a month while the company was running at close to breakeven!

The interest wasn't a big deal. It was $2,500 a month. Coughing up the $60,000 every month is what killed us. At the time of writing this, there's still $355,000 left to pay on that $600,000 note and I'm PERSONALLY liable for it. ☹

That's not a position you ever want to be in. Debt is for growth. Debt is not to save your business. If you have enough of a war chest in terms of cash, you'll never be tempted to take debt to try to save a fatally wounded animal. It's less painful and more humane to just put it down.

In the next chapter, I'll talk about how even one mis-hire can cost you as much as sucking out $2 million in distributions from your business.

FREE BONUS VIDEOS

Want to discover breakthrough strategies on how to mitigate business risk *and* grow you're business faster than you ever imagined?

WARNING: This is like nothing you've seen before. These videos are a little weird.

After clicking the link below and opting in, you'll get immediate access to my series of Business Growth Acceleration videos.

http://profitswami.com/bookbonus

As you watch each video you'll discover unorthodox cutting-edge strategies, tactics, and tools that will allow you to smash through barriers holding your business back. Helping you achieve the success and recognition you deserve.

CHAPTER 4

Hiring & Firing

The Nightmare Hire

Back in November 2012, our sales were shooting up rapidly and it dawned on us we needed to hire a sales person. At that time, my partner and I thought, *"OK. Well, let's hire an affiliate manager."*Because our strategy at that time was to drive sales through affiliates.

Affiliates are basically commission-only hired guns. They either use landing pages you provide them or create their own. Then they use various strategies, tactics, and tricks to drive traffic to your site. We give them a cut of the sales they generate for us.

Now a typical affiliate will only make a few sales a day. However, if you have an army of affiliates pushing traffic for you, the sales add up FAST.

Now, in hindsight, trying to work directly with affiliates was a *horrible* strategy.

We'll talk more about strategy in the next chapter. Let's go back to hiring...

So we were looking to hire an affiliate manager. We posted on a bunch of job sites. We even ran a LinkedIn ad!

I ripped off a job description for an affiliate manager someone else had written, and modified it for our needs. I even *required* people write and submit an essay along with their resume.

We had no idea what we were doing. We failed to work with a real HR person and didn't put a real hiring process in place.

We got a guy to reply to our ad. He sounded really impressive.

We did an interview through Google Hangout. It turns out this guy was, at one point, ranked number 74 in the world in poker! That really impressed us. Now don't ask me what that has to do with being a good affiliate manager. The answer is NOTHING.

His credentials looked really impressive. I checked his references (that I later discovered were his wife and his two best friends!). Everything looked really impressive. Fifteen minutes into the interview, we hired the guy on the spot.

I know, real smart.

Hey, he sounded good! We liked the guy because he was a former entrepreneur. He had a lot of sales experience.

We just went with our gut. As you keep reading, you'll discover why you should *NEVER go with your gut when hiring, if you don't have a formal process in place to properly vet people first.*

When you typically hire a sales person, you set up quotas, targets, expectations, reporting, etc. We didn't do any of that. He was our buddy, and he was going to help us drive sales.

In the beginning, everything seemed fine. He was just getting started. He was getting up to speed on the business. He was learning everything he could. We cut him some slack, wouldn't you?

He tagged along on industry conferences we attended. He also started calling a lot of companies. He started making lots of contacts. Putting them all in a lead database.

He seemed to be doing a lot of activity. **However, we weren't monitoring what he was *actually* doing, and what type of results he was actually producing. Colossal mistake.**

Activity does not equal results.

51

Important Lesson

The biggest dangers can pop up in your business when your business is actually doing really well, because it's easy to turn a blind eye to the danger signs when money is pouring in.

However, when your business is doing poorly, it's like a shoreline receding. All the rocks pop up as the water washes away. You suddenly get a crystal clear picture of all the shit going on *beneath the surface*. Your eyes bulge out and your jaw hits the floor. By this time, it's often too late to undo all the damage. I'll talk more about how to avoid such a calamity later.

Our sales did happen to go up during his first 6 months with us. It turned out that almost all of those sales came out from just one source. A source that I had found the year before that he had virtually nothing to do with.

Our affiliate manager did help us improve our monetization. He did do some things right. I was so impressed with how he had improved our CLV (customer lifetime value) that I gave him a promotion to Director of sales. I later discovered what he had done was a trivial accomplishment.

Then, really foolishly, I promote him to VP of sales, within six months. The worst part was the position came with a lavish severance package. Luckily, we legally got out of paying him the severance because we end up terminating him *for cause*.

After hiring him as an affiliate manager, after giving him 2 promotions all the way up to VP of sales within 6 months, we fired him 6 months later!

As the saying goes, hire slow, fire fast. Well in this case it was NOT fast enough.

It became apparent, by the end of 2013, that hiring this guy had been one of *the worst mistakes that we had ever made.*

Our growth strategy at the time was to build relationships with and drive our sales through:

1. Affiliate networks
2. Ad networks
3. Advertising agencies

Our "VP of Sales" could not convince agencies or ad networks to take our money and run advertising for us?!? No matter who he talked to, people just turned him down left and right. He was HORRIBLE at sales.

On top of that he even shut down ad networks that we were running *profitably*. That is, the few ad networks that reluctantly agreed to work with him.

I keep asking myself, *"Why can't he convince ad agencies and networks to do business with us? Aren't these companies the ones that are supposed to be pitching us, and not the other way around?"*

Then it hit me.

Be wary of hiring a professional poker player as a sales person. That may sound strange. You'd think they'd be really good at sales. Here's why they may not be.

Because our sales guywas super paranoid of everyone and everything. Everyone had a hidden agenda and was out to screw our company. He was always trying to figure out the angle. Just like a poker pro, trying to outwit and out bluff his opponent! When you're constantly suspicious of people, it *rubs off*. People can feel it.

Everyone was the enemy out to get us. Is it any wonder no one wanted to work with him?

Now, I'm not saying all poker pros are paranoid. This one was.

His paranoia got so delusional that he accused our top advertiser of sabotaging our account for the benefit of a competitor with an ALL CAPS EMAIL.

He also tainted the relationship between me and my business partner. He almost turned us against each other. Every time I made a decision he didn't like, he would poison my business partner against me.

He'd tell my partner why he didn't agree with me: *"They're out to get us. We can't trust 'em. We can't do business with 'em. Amit can't see it."*

It all came down to his bat shit paranoia. He also spread his paranoia to everyone in the company. He was persuasive. **He had almost everyone, including me, believing that all our vendors, advertisers, and channel partners were secretly working against us.** Attempting to steal our market share, or align themselves with a competitor against us!

I made the very painful decision of firing him in December 2013. However, the damage done was irreparable.

Our business was now in shambles. He had left our business tottering at the brink of bankruptcy. *What's scary is we didn't know it until after the fact, when we discovered he was fudging our daily profits sheet to show more gross profits than we actually had, by about $5,000/day!*

I blew a gasket. I was hoping mad. My face was redder than a blood orange.

We had an arrangement with him where he got paid a percentage of the gross profits of the company. The higher the gross profits were, the more he got paid. **He chose to exclude certain expense numbers from the gross profits, so he could get paid more.** That's the straw that broke the camel's back. We decided we had to fire him ASAP.

KPIs, Metrics, and the Health of Your Business

Your KPIs (key performance indicators) or metrics are specific numbers that you track on a monthly, weekly, daily basis to monitor the health of your business. Daily gross profits was a critical metric that we followed. It told us, on a daily basis, whether our advertising spend was producing a positive ROI for us. If I hadn't caught how our sales guy had fudged our daily gross profits numbers Boost could have crashed and burned within a matter of months.

We had a false gauge of the state of our business. It was really scary.

By inflating our daily gross profits, he was inflating his commissions and stealing from the company. He also gave us a false sense of security about the health of Boost.

How to Bat 1000 at Hiring

It's estimated that a mis-hire can cost anywhere from $500,000 to $1.5 million dollars (depending on your source). I can tell you that our mis-hire cost us *millions of dollars*. It was an absolute disaster. It took months of focused effort to mend all the broken relationships and to get the company back into profitability.

I didn't make the same mistake twice. I found a replacement for him, a guy named Pete, who turned out to be a superstar. I made him Director of sales within 6 months. He was instrumental in turning the company sales around.

Recommendation

Read a book called "Who" by Geoff Smart and Randy Street. It succinctly covers the topgrading methodology for hiring. Think of topgrading as a way to guarantee that you'll hire A-players 90% of the time.

Sounds too good to be true? Until we tried it and ended up with an entire team of A-players!

Having a really rigorous process in place for hiring (like topgrading) was a game changer. You have to realize realizing that it's very easy to hire people and it's very difficult to fire people - very difficult.

The biggest breakthrough was implementing a REAL hiring process. Run by someone who knew what they were doing. It all started after we brought on a highly experienced Director of HR. We also followed a process very similar to Topgrading™. I'll talk more about this later.

Slow and Steady Wins the Race

We ended up really slowing down the hiring process. *Taking three to four months to hire somebody, even if we badly needed that role filled.* It turned out to be a really good decision.

Setting up KPIs to carefully monitor the performance of new hires was also a game changer, *especially for sales people*. Because the really friendly and cool sales guy you just hired is NOT your buddy and never should be. He's there to do a specific task. And if he's unwilling or unable to do that task, then you need to can him, FAST.

Hiring is a Tricky Thing

If you hire too slowly, you're going to bottleneck the growth of your company. It could even kill your company if you have hockey stick growth. You're understaffed. And you can't fulfill orders that are pouring in.

Slow hiring can feel like business constipation, especially when you have a product launch delayed 2 months because you badly needed another full-time GUI designer.

I gotta tell you, 2 months of constipation is a painful thing. Especially when everyone in the company can feel it.

We'd have business constipation a couple times a year. We sucked it up and waited a couple of months to get the *right person in place.*

Hiring too quickly can also create serious problems.

We ended up over hiring a bit in Poland. We had a big team: web developers, Windows developers, QA people, designers, and even an office manager. At our peak, we had a team of 13 full-time employees in our Poland office.

We hit a point where we didn't have enough work for the Poland team. They were getting restless. These guys were A-players and if they were not being challenged, they would jump ship. I was forced to come up with new projects for them to work on. Just to keep them busy and challenged.

57

However, I wasn't losing too much sleep over Poland because it only cost us between $2,000 - $3,000/month per employee. We had a QA intern that cost us only $3/hr!

If you know what you're doing, building an overseas team can save you a bundle. It can also bring on some highly talented and super motivated people onto your team. Always a plus. I talk more about how to do this in my free video series.

So what's the secret to hiring the right number of people at the right time?

Proper Planning Prevents Poor Performance

I know, cliché right?

Planning and growth projections are the key to striking the right balance of hiring the right number of people at the right time. You've got to get GOOD at predicting what your company will look like 6 months, 1 year, 2 years, even 5 years from now.

Ask yourself this question: If you're $500,000 company right now, what's your company going to look like when it's at $5 million dollars? How many people are you going to have? What positions are you going to hold? What's your org. chart going to look like? You've got to plan that out.

A solid plan and growth projections, *put together properly,* will rocket your business forward, without costly pit stops. *Imagine being able to start the hiring process for a key position 3-4 months before you need to fill the position.* If executed correctly, you'll be able to accelerate the growth of your business and build the *momentum of a freight train,* all while keeping a lid on payroll costs.

Having a plan and growth projections is not enough. You need to keep a constant pulse on your business and adjust your projects and hiring needs as market conditions change.

That's where quarterly and monthly meeting with your executive team and board meetings come in. These meetings allow you to look at your business from a bird's eye view. It gives you the chance to work ON the business, and not IN the business.

The Cash Flow Trap

It's easy to hire when the money is pouring in and you're sitting on a mountain of cash. It's an all you can eat buffet, how can you say no?

It's easy to fall into the "happily ever after" trap. If things are going well and the business is blowing up, it's fun to go on a ~~spending~~ investing spree.

Just keep in mind, businesses have ups and downs as they grow. If the cash flow and the profits you're making right now are fragile, especially if they're coming predominantly from one source (which can often be the case in the beginning) then going on a hiring spree can be a dangerous game.

Assume that whatever cashflow you have now can crash and burn tomorrow. If your sales take a 25 percent dip, can you still make payroll without sweating bullets?

Don't get me wrong. If your business is growing fast, chances are that you will need to hire more people. Just don't go overboard.

FREE BONUS VIDEOS

Want to discover breakthrough strategies on how to mitigate business risk *and* grow you're business faster than you ever imagined?

WARNING: This is like nothing you've seen before. These videos are a little weird.

After clicking the link below and opting in, you'll get immediate access to my series of Business Growth Acceleration videos.

http://profitswami.com/bookbonus

As you watch each video you'll discover unorthodox cutting-edge strategies, tactics, and tools that will allow you to smash through barriers holding your business back. Helping you achieve the success and recognition you deserve.

CHAPTER 5

Strategy & Entrepreneurial ADD

Two Types of Businesses

Strategy is what differentiates you from your competition. It's the series of tradeoffs your business makes. While it may make your business weak in some areas, it allows you to completely dominate in others.

Operational Effectiveness versus Strategy

Strategy is separating yourself from your competitors with a series of trade offs and different activities. On the other hand, operational effectiveness is how well you perform similar tasks compared to your competitor.

For you smarty pant out there, you'll quickly pick up on that fact I'm primarily talking about operational effectiveness in the chapter, and calling it strategy. I'm well aware of the difference.

The ugly truth is that most smaller companies out there drop the ball on operational effectiveness. If you're not continually improving your operational effectiveness, you're dead in the water as it is. I'll explain why as you read on.

In my opinion, you have to get your operational effectiveness right first, before you start worrying about putting a game changing strategy in place. You need to learn how to walk first, before you can run.

When you finally nail your strategy, you'll be whistling and skipping along while effortlessly bringing in fat margins and competitor-crushing cashflow. However, if you don't have a good strategy in place, you're not going to survive long-term. Instead, you'll get eaten alive.

There are two types of businesses:

1. **The Copycat Business** (my personal favorite), where you're basically selling a product or service that already exists in the marketplace. Your product could be a commodity like bar soap or toilet paper, but doesn't have to be (I'll explain why later).

2. **The Innovation Business**, where you have a highly innovative product, and that innovation *is your strategy*. However, innovation alone is a *short-term strategy*, unless you have a patent or a product or service that is almost impossible to rip off. Competitors will eventually come out of the woodworks and start nipping at your heels.

Boost was a copycat business. We sold PC optimizers and other PC utility products. Most businesses are copycat business, and that's **my favorite type of business** for a couple reasons:

1. There's a proven market for your product or service
2. You have successful competitors you can ~~rip off~~ dissect, analyze, and model.
3. Your chances of success are FAR greater. You may never be the next Facebook. However, you still can have kickass business that makes a big impact that provides you the lifestyle you've always dreamed of.

At Boost, we had to think long and hard about our strategy. We did some things right, and we did some things horribly wrong.

For starters, we realized that the biggest key to dominating our space was focusing all our efforts on driving online sales because my business partner and I have both been super affiliates promoting PC optimizers in the past. So it made total sense just to leverage our core strength, which was online marketing.

We said to ourselves, "*Here's what we're going to do: we're going to create the best converting PC optimizer and the best performing online sales funnel in the market. Then, we're going to work with channel partners, affiliate networks, ad networks, affiliates, to drive an avalanche of sales for us.*"

That pretty much summed up our strategy. And it worked like gangbusters, for a while anyway. However, we were missing one *critical* component in our strategy. This missing component led to Boost's inevitable downfall. I'll get more into that later, for now you may be wondering how we went from...

---

0 to 8-Figures with our Flagship Product in 18 months?

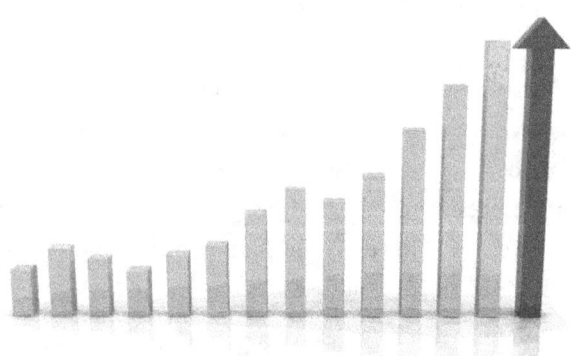

We focused our effort on creating the highest converting product flow, landing pages, and cart pages. We obsessively growth-hacked the whole sales funnel until we were blue in the face from split testing. **We ended up**

increasing our conversion rate by over 300% in a matter of 12 months.

We systematically tested our product, identified and repaired bugs, did rigorous A/B split testing, tested different versions of the product and landing page over and over again. We discovered some really crazy stuff that skyrocketed our sales conversion and allowing us to profitability buy more and more advertising.

We went from a nobody to the talk of the industry. We did all of this just by consistently growth hacking.

Well, growth hacking plus expanding our sales channels. *Realize this though*: **higher conversions allow you to outspend your competitors, buy more traffic (or leads), and tilt the entire marketplace in your favor.**

This is true whether you're doing cold emails and cold calling for b2b leads or banners ads to directly sell a consumer product. If you convert more cold calls and cold emails to sales than your competitor, all with a lower churn rate, what do you think will happen over time?

That's right, you will completely dominate, even if your product is almost identical to your competitors. Start fanatically working day and night to improve the conversion rate and ROI on your sales and marketing, and watch what happens to your business. If done properly, you can quickly transform your business from a timid kitten to roaring lion.

We launched our flagship product in May of 2012. By the end of 2013, we generated $11.6 million in revenue – in 2013 alone. The following year was rough; however, we still had a $10 million run rate right before we were sued by the FTC.

Yes, it can happen that *fast*. However, if there are any holes in your strategy, things can start falling apart just as fast.

The Hyper-Responsive Beachhead & Black Lambos

The biggest faux pas in our strategy was failing to drill down and really dissect our competition. Ask yourself this question: **who in your space can afford to pay cash for a black lambo?**

If you can't immediately answer that question, then you've got some homework to do. If you can, your next step is to study this company inside out:

- ❖ Where are they buying their traffic or leads from?
- ❖ How and where are they advertising?
- ❖ What industry/market segments are they going after? If it's a B2C company, what demographics are they targeting?
- ❖ Become their customer (if possible). Analyze their ENTIRE sales, onboarding, and customer/lead engagement process.

We had competitors literally tracking EVERY change we made to our landing pages. They would quickly follow suit and copy what we were doing.

Using the right market research tools, you can strip your competition bare. You can see almost everything they're doing behind the scenes.

The #1 insight you want to dig up when analyzing your competition is their hyper-responsive beachhead.

What the heck is that?

Every market has a segment that hauls in a disproportionate amount of profits. This market segment may account for maybe 10 percent of the total market, but they may account for *50 percent of the profitability from that market.* This is your hyper-responsive beachhead. If you haven't found yours, then guess what? You're fighting for table scraps.

When our sales slowed down in 2014, it finally forced us to do a black lambo analysis in our market. Here are the top 5 countries our top competitor is advertising in (courtesy of Alexa.com):

Country	Percent of Visitors	Rank in Country
Brazil	10.3%	2,847
Japan	8.6%	5,000
France	7.5%	3,038
Germany	4.9%	5,831
Russia	4.7%	7,002

The US is NOT even in the top 5?!? Here's what's shocking: we were predominantly advertising in the US, with a bit of traffic coming from UK and AU. **After further analysis, it finally hit us that our margins in US were razor thin, compared to what we could be getting in other countries, particularly non-English speaking countries!**

The hard truth was that advertising in the US was very expensive, because the US is the biggest consumer market in the world. That means massive sales volume and cutthroat competition. *It's an absolute blood bath.*

Compared to advertising in Germany, France, Japan, and Brazil, we were paying a king's ransom to acquire customers in the US.

All this time we had been beating our heads against the wall trying to improve our margins, when we could have advertised in non-English speaking countries and absolutely cleaned house. We would have paid much less for advertising, faced much less competition, and enjoyed fat margins to follow. ☹

Entrepreneurial ADD and Shiny Object Syndrome

There's something called entrepreneurial ADD or shiny object syndrome. It's like a dog spotting a squirrel. It completely loses its focus, stops what it's doing, and suddenly redirects all its attention and energy towards the squirrel.

I'm sure this has never happened to you. However, it happens to the best of us. You come up with a 'breakthrough idea' for a totally new product (or service). Or maybe even a new business.

That could be a gigantic strategic mistake. Why? Listen, if you have something that's working like gangbusters right now, by chasing the new breakthrough idea, *you're now suddenly diverting a huge amount of money and resources into doing something completely different.* You're pulling your company away from your core product or service. **You could be smashing a wrecking ball through your company if you're not careful.**

Let me elaborate…

Let's say you do have a flagship product and it's doing great and you're now thinking, *"OK, well, we're kind of working on product A, let's work on product B."* You suddenly shift half your resources into creating product B and marketing product B. Let's say a year later product B doesn't quite pan out.

68

Here's what happens overtime: you start realizing, *"Oh my God, our product A sales are going down. Our competitors are overtaking us on product A. And product B was a complete dud. Now our business is suddenly in a downswing!"*

How did this happen? **Because you focused your attention away from your core competencies, away from your strengths, to try to do something completely different. Huge mistake.**

You're like, *"Oh yeah, well Google does this. Microsoft does it. All these other companies, big companies are doing it."* Well, they've got a billion dollars in the bank. They can do that. You're a small company. You need to focus on your core competency. You need to focus on your product A. Make it the best it can possibly be. Continually improving it. Continually work to get more market share.

The Payment Processor Pitfall

I was majorly guilty of chasing that new shiny object that promised even more fortune and glory! This was especially true when things were going GREAT.

We thought to ourselves, *"OK. We're doing great. How about we create our own payment processor? How about we start our own affiliate network? We can really dominate then!"*

We wasted 6 months trying to build our own shopping cart and affiliate network, only to throw our hands up in defeat. We were attempting to start a new business in a space we know very little about. It required pivoting our focus away from our **core strengths: developing and marketing software PC utility products.**

It was a fool's errand. It was not worth the effort. It was not our business model.

More than the direct cost of attempting to build our own cart and affiliate network, *the opportunity cost was devastating.* It's time and resources we could have spent improving our existing technology, expanding our sales channels, growth hacking, etc. Instead of improving our core business, we started to fall behind. Not surprising, sales started to drop.

By deviating from our core competencies, we took a *big hit financially.* I began to panic and realign my whole team to focus on our core strengths and we:

1. Finally launched a new version of our PC product.
2. Overhauled our tracking technology. This allowed us to open up new (very profitable) sales channels.
3. Growth hacked our way to another 30% increase in sales conversion.
4. Etc., etc.

Within 4 months, our sales and profits massively rebounded.

A Couple Caveats

You may be squirming in your seat right now as you're reading this, and you may be thinking: *"But Amit, I read that to grow my business from $1million to $10million I need to grow a line of product and services. You're full of shit!"*

You're right. Calm down, keep reading and let me elaborate.

There are situations where it makes sense to build a line of products or services. Here are the criteria you must meet first:

1. **Strong position in the market with your current offering.**

   You've found your product/market fit. It's been selling well for years. *You have lots of money in the bank. And you have enough staff to develop and market a new product or service.*

2. **The new offering is something that compliments your main product.** You can sell the new offering to your existing customer base. (i.e. Your main product is square widgets, and your new product is a round widget.)

3. You've validated that your **existing customer base wants to buy the new gizmo** you're going to create. There are lots of ways of doing this.

By following the above criteria, you're dramatically minimizing your risk because:

- For starters, you're not sucking away too many resources from your main money maker. After all, it's paying the bills and keeping the lights on. You want to nurture your firstborn.

- You've optimized your main sales channels well enough that you can leverage everything you've learned to sell your new product or service. Since their complimentary products, you can use the same strategies to market your new product.

- You have a huge list of customers ready and waiting to buy your new product. Sales from your product launch to your existing customer base alone could pay for the entire cost of development.

- You can sell your new product to every new customer on the backend. This will seriously bump up your CLV (customer lifetime value).

Boost was already selling a third party antivirus product to our customers on our backend successfully. It made total sense for us to spend a year developing an antivirus product *because we knew we could immediately start making money with it.*

Antivirus products were in the same category of products that we had already developed. It was a product our customers were ready to snap up. It increased our CLV. It opened up new marketing channels and opportunities for us. And it improved our brand since now we could position ourselves as a security company, instead of a PC optimization company.

Those are the types of strategic decisions you really need to put some thought into.

Even while our development team was working away creating our Antivirus application, we still continued to improve our PC optimizer product. We didn't lose sight of the fact that it was our cash cow.

Remember that all products have a lifecycle. If you're not continually improving them and releasing new major upgrades every so often, you're going to start falling behind.

Keep a Fire Lit Under Your Butt

When your business is doing well, be wary of shiny objects that can lead you astray from your true core and the purpose of your company. You must always act with a sense of urgency, even when your business is growing like a weed.

You have to act, literally, like your business is on the brink of bankruptcy every month. *This will force you to come up with new breakthroughs to keep your business growing and ahead of the pack.*

If you don't act with a sense of urgency, if you say, "*Oh, we're doing great. We're the top product on the market. We're kicking everyone's butt.*" The second you become complacent, your business starts to slowly die. And your competitors start to *smell* weakness.

The "*OMG I need to grow my business otherwise I will go bust*" mindset will motivate you to come up with a lot of creative ideas to: grow your profitability, grow your margins, expand your sales channels and fine-tune your strategy.

When you get complacent and think you've 'arrived,' you start straying away from your core strengths. That's when things can get very dangerous.

You can lose focus, start chasing shiny objects, and straying from everything that makes your company successful in the first place. All while your competitors are nipping at your heels. Constantly improving in the background. And overtaking you in the process, while you're sitting back celebrating with your team.

Getting distracted by shiny objects is just one of many dangerous you'll face as you grow your business. In the next chapter, I talk about another danger you'll likely face when your business is doing well.

There are many facets to having a winning business strategy. I've just touched on a few ideas in this chapter. For a deeper dive in to the fine art of business strategy, watch my free video series. See the link below.

FREE BONUS VIDEOS

Want to discover breakthrough strategies on how to mitigate business risk *and* grow you're business faster than you ever imagined?

WARNING: This is like nothing you've seen before. These videos are a little weird.

After clicking the link below and opting in, you'll get immediate access to my series of Business Growth Acceleration videos.

http://profitswami.com/bookbonus

As you watch each video you'll discover unorthodox cutting-edge strategies, tactics, and tools that will allow you to smash through barriers holding your business back. Helping you achieve the success and recognition you deserve.

CHAPTER 6

The Sirens of Satisfaction

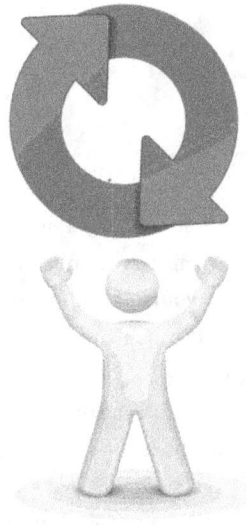

Good Enough, We've Made it

Ever thought to yourself: *"OK Good enough! Business is going great! Time to lift my foot off the gas pedal and smell the roses. We made it!"*

If I was an investor in your company and I heard you say or even suggest something like that at a board meeting, I would be running for the hills and selling my shares the first opportunity got.

Why?

Because you've just succumbed to the sirens of satisfaction. The second you believe your business is "good enough," you're on a sinking ship.

If you're having a lot of success, then I assume you are working your butt off, building and improving every aspect of the business until you got your business to the point to where it is now.

What do you think will happen when you stop doing everything that made your success in the first place?

Here's what may happen:

1. You'll get bored and distracted by a novel idea or project, and steer your company away from its core purpose.
2. You'll stop educating yourself and growing as a leader. Thinking that there's not that much more you need to learn. Think Hindenburg size ego.
3. Your team will follow suit and lose the sense of excitement and purpose they previously had. Your culture will nose dive, and morale will suffer.
4. You'll start taking out larger distributions and bonuses. After all, you've arrived, right? What's the point of keep millions in the bank! Time to cash out.
5. Your competitors will keep working away. They'll chip away at your market position. And slowly start overtaking you.

Get the picture?

The Slide

Now what's really scary is that depending on your market you could operate happily in the "Good enough - we've made it" mindset for YEARS before your business starts to slide and fall apart.

The good news is if your business is at this point right now, it may not be too late to turn things around.

In 2013 Boost had its best year. Profits were pouring in so fast our heads were spinning.

We thought we had arrived. Finally, after years of struggling to just get our product created, we made it! We stopped growth hacking with the same intensity we used to. We were not working with a sense of urgency anymore.

This was around the time we tried to create our own payment processer and affiliate network that I talked about in chapter 5. As you know, this turned out to be a huge mistake. It easily set us back 6 months.

On top of this my business partner and I pulled out a LOT of money out of the company. Because we thought we had made it, pulling out a big chunk of cash to buy a house would not hurt the business.

We could not have been more wrong. By the end of 2013 our biggest sales channel had completely dried up. On top of this we were getting hammered by DDoS attacks (denial of service attacks that bring your website and your business to a stretching halt). We could barely keep our website up, let alone make a profit.

Reality hit me like a bucket of ice water. As I mentioned in Chapter 5, after 4 months of concentrated efforts our new director of sales and I finally got Boost back in profitability.

Constant and Never Ending Improvement

The best way to keep the sirens of satisfaction at bay is always operating with a sense of urgency and constant, never ending, improvement.

Every company should have an unspoken core value of continuous improvement.

And I'm not just talking about growth hacking. I'm talking about improving all areas of your business: HR, legal, accounting, sales and marketing, operations, strategy, etc.

If you're not constantly improving. If you're not constantly putting tremendous pressure on yourself. If you don't have a sense of urgency about:

1. Growing your business,
2. Growing your sales,
3. Growing your profits,
4. Growing your team,
5. Improving your business in every way.

Then guess what? *You're dead in the water. If not now, then eventually you'll slide, crash, and burn.*

You have to be continually behaving as if your business is on the verge of bankruptcy. Build your business with the sense of urgency that, *"Hey, if we don't find something to improve this week, this month, this day, then we're going to be out of business next month."*

You Must Grow First, Before Your Business Grows

Continuous improvement also means continuously growing *as a leader*. What are you doing on a regular basis to build your leadership skills?

You might be running a one million dollar company, right now. You're going to have to be a *different person* to successfully run a $5 million or $10 million dollar company.

> If you're not growing as a leader as you grow your business, you'll become the greatest bottleneck for your business' growth.

Continuous improvement comes from the inside before it manifests on the outside. It's a mindset.

Developing leadership skills is more than improving your ability to lead, motivate, and manage others. As your business grows, you'll need to learn how to identify and develop leaders within your organization.

Once your team really starts to grow, you'll have to train and develop a group of 6-8 frontline managers (your direct reporters) who will have people under them *that they manage*. Because you don't want more than 6-10 direct reporters at a time, otherwise you'll get overwhelmed. You won't be able to give everyone the attention they need.

FREE BONUS VIDEOS

Want to discover breakthrough strategies on how to mitigate business risk *and* grow you're business faster than you ever imagined?

WARNING: This is like nothing you've seen before. These videos are a little weird.

After clicking the link below and opting in, you'll get immediate access to my series of Business Growth Acceleration videos.

http://profitswami.com/bookbonus

As you watch each video you'll discover unorthodox cutting-edge strategies, tactics, and tools that will allow you to smash through barriers holding your business back. Helping you achieve the success and recognition you deserve.

CHAPTER 7

Please Sign Along the Dotted Line...

The Legal Fortress

I'm not a huge fan of perusing through business contracts. Frankly, it's boring. I'm an entrepreneur. I'm a visionary. I like seeing the big picture. I don't like going through line after line and page after page of legalese.

It makes my head spin.

However, I quickly learned how important it was to have a *solid contract* in place for all your business dealings, *especially for the big deals.*

Checking off a box in a contract for a $20/month service is one thing. However, if you're signing a contract for something where you're making a five or six–figure commitment per year, then you need to *read every line until your eyes are bloodshot, AND have your attorney look it over.*

A good business attorney is really good at looking at all the risks that your business could be exposed to, and protecting you from those risks. *Those risks could be catastrophic, do not underestimate them.*

A good attorney can suck your wallet dry, costing $300 to $400 an hour. *However, they are worth every cent.* They will help you identify all the dirty little tricks, completely one-sided terms, and nasty restrictions hidden in the contract. Those risks are frighteningly real and should not be ignored. Point in fact; signing one bad contract can **chop down the valuation of your company.**

Boost spent close to half a million on legal fees in 3 years. It was money well spent.

Having an attorney pour over all your legal contracts to make them air tight is like creating a legal fortress around your company. It will protect you when a business deal goes south – like the time I lost $125,000!

Working with an attorney on contract negotiations requires extreme patience; a deal that could be live tomorrow could take another month to get done. One month is an eternity for a fast growing company – you'll be ready to jump out of your skin.

Contract negotiations also need to be done *properly.* If you're not careful and your attorney is too aggressive with the contract changes, then you could seriously piss off the other party. The entire deal could collapse before your eyes.

Business Terms that Bite You in the Ass

Read over the business terms of any contract you sign, as if you're reading over a contract from Vinny the loan shark. Because they can sneak stuff in the business terms that are pretty nasty. You need to read the contract really carefully and *clarify exactly what the payment structure is.*

Your attorney will not review the business terms. That's your job. Make sure you take it seriously.

Taking a microscope, and reading the business terms line by line is *especially* important if you're working with contracts where there are 6-month minimum to 12-month minimum commitments with monthly expectation of payments. I'm not talking about $10/month. I'm talking in the $1000s per month. Think enterprise level agreements.

The Agency Train Wreck

We worked with an AdWords agency (whose name I won't mention). I glossed over the business terms, and completely missed that there was a minimum of $20,000 a month commitment.

That's steep price for AdWords management. It only makes sense if they do a REALLY good job. They'd absolutely have to kill it. However, if you're going to sign a contract with an agency that's $20,000 a month minimum, *you've got to read the fine print really carefully and make sure that if they mess up, you are not liable for paying that $20,000 a month for 6 months, to the tune of $120,000.*

I signed the contract, not realizing there was a minimum commitment of $20,000 a month **no matter what they did**. Secondly, there was a very weak out clause in the contract.

I bit my tongue and kicked myself when I realized the minimum commitment was $20,000 a month. I crossed my fingers and prayed that this agency was worth its salt.

Things went downhill from there...

After about 3 weeks of working on our AdWords account, they *completely* wrecked it. They drove our spend up to $30,000 a day with no increase in sales, destroying our entire account. Luckily, I caught the massive spend jump immediately and paused the account.

I had to manually rebuild the AdWords account myself. That alone cost the company about $100,000.

On top of this, the agency had the gall to demand payment for the remainder of their contract. I said, *"I'm not paying. This is bullshit. I'm not* *going to pay you guys for $20,000 a month when you wrecked our Google account. We're terminating the relationship on cause."* I was hopping mad.

We ended up negotiating with them for one final $20,000 payment spread out over 5 months. IN exchange, they signed a contract agreeing they would not sue us for the $120,000 owed per our agreement.

The Payment Processer Fist Fight

Another deal that got ugly was with a payment processor, where I didn't read the business terms carefully enough. Our attorney had reviewed and negotiated the legal terms.

Again, I missed the minimum commitment of $30,000 a month in sales commissions based on the assumption that we would be generating at least 12,000 sales a month and around $800,000- $1,000,000 a month in sales, out of which they would receive $30,000.

However, they would charge $30,000 minimum, *regardless* of whether we made five sales in the month or whether we made 50,000 sales. Bad idea agreeing to that. Of course, they assured me this was "standard" in the industry.

Yeah right.

To add fuel to the fire, their shopping cart did not convert as well as our existing shopping cart. It turned out to be a total disaster, but we still had this contract where we owed them a massive amount of money.

There wasn't a strong enough escape clause in the contract for us to get out of it. So by the time we were about to battle it out with fists flying, we ended up going bust. So it turned out to be a moot point.

Before signing any long-term contracts, 6 to 12 months with large monthly payment commitments, you have to make sure the contract is set up in a way where:

1. You can do a limited test run with the company for a 60-day period before you make a bigger commitment
2. There's an escape clause in a contract so that you can terminate the relationship with a 30-day notice in case shit hits the fan.

Really make sure you take a few days to sleep on every major contract before you sign off. Make sure it's absolutely something you want to do and you're absolutely confident it's going to work.

Better yet, make major contract board decisions. That forces you to sell the idea to your board. And if can't convince your board, then you've got a problem.

$125,000 Lesson: Beware of Outsource Software Development

When my business partner and I first started Boost, we got ripped off to the tune of $125,000. It almost put us under. We had just started. We were not making any money and the company was extremely fragile. I was self-funding the company. Putting my own money into it to keep it afloat.

We thought to ourselves, "*OK. We need a flagship product. We need to hire developers to build our product.*" We found a development company out of California. The guy sounded really professional. He was really charismatic and sounded like he'd be the perfect guy for the job.

He claimed his team could create an amazing product for us. He even said he could help us market it. He wined us and dined us. Within 2 weeks, we signed a contract with this guy. We did not have an attorney look it over. *We even gave him the right to bill our credit card automatically every month!*

Initially he said, "*Oh, wait. Let me create a small product for you guys that will only cost you around $7,000 to $10,000.*" So he did that. He delivered on it. It was actually a pretty good product, but not perfect.

So he had hooked us at that point. He delivered on a small project and now he was ready to lure us in for the kill. He understood the power of commitment and consistency. He knew he had us.

After the small project was complete, we started working on the main product, our PC optimizer. That's when he started billing us $25,000 a month, month after month. No milestones. No deliverables. No functional spec or project plan. He would just keep telling us: *"OK, we're almost there."* Occasionally he would share screen shots.

He went on and on, *"Oh, we're almost there. I'll have something to show you in a week. I'll have something to show you in two weeks,"* and kept pushing it off. At one point, after racking up $125,000 in expenses, I just went to him and said, *"Hey, we're out of money. We have to stop. We can't continue any longer."*

I'm embarrassed to talk about this. I could not believe how naïve I was back then. ☹

I didn't know what to think at that point. I suspected something was wrong but couldn't put my finger on it. Then I went to an industry conference and I talked to somebody I highly respect. I told him about our experience. I said, *"I have a bad feeling about it. He hasn't delivered. We spent $125,000. We don't know what's going on?"*

I mentioned the name of the guy we'd been working with. He said, *"Oh yeah, that guy. That guy scammed about seven other people in our industry, including myself. I had to threaten to sue him before he agreed to complete our app."*

I was jaw slacked. Fist clenched. I was angry and shocked at the same time.

I almost had a panic attack, realizing we had been taken by this basically professional con man to the tune of $125,000. I went back and talked to my attorney immediately.

Because I did not have my attorney look over the contract –I just signed it carte blanche – I had virtually no recourse. We didn't have a solid case.

That was a $125,000 learning lesson that I would *never ever* repeat again. We were not making any money. Losing money at this stage was catastrophic for our company, and me personally, since it was all my money! We came *really* close to closing our doors. ☹

It took us six months to recover from the $125,000 loss. Fortunately, we did manage to get some revenue coming in by selling a whitelabel product. That kept us afloat.

We made a second attempt at developing our flagship product. We hired 2 contractors who said they could do the job. They were a referral.

This time we did it right.

We had our attorney write up the contract that set out measurable milestones for development. All for a fixed cost of $50,000. We paid them at the end of each milestone, with delivery of the latest code. We also started with a detailed project plan and functional specs of the application.

We made an upfront payment. Additional payments were sent out only after:

1. A new development milestone was hit
2. We did a call detailing the progress, plus a code review
3. We officially signed off on the changes for that milestone

If they didn't hit the milestone, they didn't get paid. That was the bottom line.

We withheld the final payment (a huge chunk of change) until we gave them a thumbs up on the final product.

The good news is that we got our final product this time. ☺

However, it ended up being a disaster. It was a mess. It was crawling with bugs. Every other link you clicked on would cause the program to crash.

We ended up paying these guys the full $50,000 we owed them. They got 95% of the job done. I had to search long and hard on Elance to find 2 more developers who could get the job done.

These 2 new guys, Mariusz and Roberto, who were from Europe, turned out to be rock stars and became permanent members of the Boost team. We eventually fired our initial two developers. Mariusz and Roberto completely took over.

Sorry to digress here, the story of how I built our rockstar in-house development team is something I'll get into later!

Here's the takeaway...

When hiring an outsourced development team to do a large project, you want to structure it as a fixed cost, milestone-based project with a *strong binding* legal agreement behind it. This will guarantee that you:

1. Minimize your risk you
2. Get your project completed and in a reasonable time period
3. And that you don't get jerked around or cheat.

No conman will sign such an agreement. Speaking of conmen...

Exposing a Conman

My business partner and I were trying lots of different types of business opportunities when we initially started the company. We didn't have a lot of focus back then, and hey, we were just hustling to try to make some quick cash.

WARNING

It's generally a really bad idea to stray away from your core business and start other ventures. If you try to chase 2 rabbits, you'll catch neither! Building a company requires *complete dedication and focus.* You gotta put your whole heart and soul into it. Anything less and you're bound for failure.

The only exception is if you're pivoting your business, because things are quickly going nowhere fast with your core business.

Anyway, we had this whole business plan worked out for an annuity lead generation business. We even had some contacts in the annuity business that were anxious to sell the leads we would generate. Ultimately, it didn't end up working out because we discovered our new business partner was a conman!

We went back and forth with him on the contract. He tried to squeeze us for every penny he could. He snuck stuff into the contract to increase his percentage. He pulled every dirty little trick in the book.

He thought we were dupes. We pushed back pretty hard. We had our attorney go through everything. We were ready to sign the contract, and then literally three days before we're about to sign the contract, he changed his company name.

He set up a shell company and quietly slipped it into the contract. His real company was a 3-letter acronym, and his fake shell company was also a 3-letter acronym, WITH similar letters! It was nearly impossible to detect that he had swapped out his real company with a fake shell company in the contract. Sneaky Devil.

Luckily, our attorney is super-sharp, and she picked up on the fact that he pulled a classic bait and switch. We immediately backed out.

It cost about $10,000 in legal fees to do all the paperwork for the annuity agreement. However, had we not done that, we would have signed with him and *we would have sunk $100,000 minimum before we realized this guy was conning us.*

$10,000 in legal fees saved us $100,000. That's a 1000% ROI.

FREE BONUS VIDEOS

Want to discover breakthrough strategies on how to mitigate business risk *and* grow you're business faster than you ever imagined?

WARNING: This is like nothing you've seen before. These videos are a little weird.

After clicking the link below and opting in, you'll get immediate access to my series of Business Growth Acceleration videos.

http://profitswami.com/bookbonus

As you watch each video you'll discover unorthodox cutting-edge strategies, tactics, and tools that will allow you to smash through barriers holding your business back. Helping you achieve the success and recognition you deserve.

CHAPTER 8

Relationships

Liked & Respected

In this chapter, I want to talk about within your team. As you read on, you'll also see the consequences of becoming friends with your employees. It's a dangerous proposition. You could end up getting your heart pulled out and stomped on. Worse, you're endangering your company.

As a leader, you're tiptoeing on a tightrope, balancing between being liked and being respected.

Let me repeat that. You want to be liked, but you also must be respected. If you get too buddy-buddy with an employee, if you become best friends, you're headed down a treacherous road. Here's a couple reasons why:

1. Losing Respect

Let's say you become BFF with one of your employees. You're watching football with them every Sunday. You're going out to the bar with them, or whatever social activities you might engage in. You're doing it all on a regular basis. After awhile, **they're not going to respect you anymore.**

They've gotten too emotionally close to you to see you as their boss, as their leader. They get to really know you, all your faults and what you're like. You may have heard that familiarity breeds contempt. Bottom line: *It's going to be hard for people on your team to respect you if you get too close to them.*

2. Emotions Cloud Your Judgment

If you become emotionally attached to people on your team, you become good friends with them, you're constantly talking to them, you develop a really strong bond with them, then *it's going to completely blind your judgment of their performance.*

It's going to cloud your judgment of whether this is the right person for the job. Whether they're doing a good job. Whether you should promote them. Whether you should fire them. And how quickly you should fire them.

3. Preferential Treatment

Becoming good friends with employees affects your ability to treat everyone fairly. And that's a critical part of being a good leader. Everyone needs to feel like they're being treated fairly. There can be no favoritism. There are *no exceptions* for anyone on the team.

Everyone follows the same rules and is held up to the same standards, *including yourself.*

I'm Not Telling You to Be a Prick

Listen, you should always be friendly with everyone. Always give them honest praise and appreciation. Give them occasional high five, knuckle thumps, elbow bumps, or whatever your company's into!

Part of being a great leader is constantly praising people, appreciating people for what they've done, and being a nice, warm, friendly person.

Being friendly is different than being friends. Being friends is something that you absolutely do not want to do with anyone that's directly reporting to you or anyone in your company for that matter. As a CEO, as a leader, you need to keep an emotional distance from *everyone* on your team.

That doesn't mean when you go to a conference together with one of your employees that you can't hang out and have fun and cut up. Or if you have an offsite team meeting that you can't be friendly with your team, and even treat them like a friend (while not getting too close).

There's a difference between an acquaintance and somebody you're seeing three or four times a week and hanging out with constantly.

Let me tell you want happened when I got too close to the first sales guy we hired...

A Gut Wrenchingly Painful Mistake

The first sales guy we hired, you know the guy we tossed out the door? Well, he became friends with me and really close friends with my business partner.

I think this was a deliberate strategy on his part. He went out of his way to reach out to me and my partner. I later discovered that he became really close to my partner, talking to him hours per day.

While my partner hours a day (wonder how much work either of them were getting done!), I traveled quite a bit with him on trips to conferences to meet vendors and channel partners.

It wasn't just business. He became a friend.

That clouded my judgment of his performance and also clouded my business partner's judgment of his performance. *It damn near capsized and sunk our business, as it caused us to delay terminating him.* We delayed firing him because of the relationship we had with him. I also showered him with unwarranted promotions and raises because of that relationship.

Firing him was gut-wrenchingly painful for both my partner and I. It's hard enough firing someone, terminating a friendship at the same time felt like being eviscerated.

The King and his Sycophants

You gotta keep your guard up at all times because just like every lord and servant who wants to be friends with the king, a lot of people on your team will want to get close to you. They're going to want to be your best friend because they know being the best friend of the boss means that they'll get special treatment, more promotions, and more raises.

And more importantly, they'll never get fired!

Once you develop a bond with somebody, it's very hard to let them go or to really look at them objectively when you're doing a performance evaluation of them and their work. That's why it's absolutely critical that you keep an emotional distance from your employees. It *can also taint the culture of your company.* I explain why below.

They're Watching Your Every Move

Your team is looking at every single move that you're making. They're watching every single word that you're saying. Watching every action that you're taking. If you show up late to work 30 minutes every day, that leaves a massively negative impression on your team. They're not going to say anything. They'll never say anything to you.

Let's say you're having lunch with the one employee every day. They're getting special attention, and you're hanging with them a lot. Guess what? You're giving them special treatment. That's going to reflect negatively on you.

Your team is going to watch every little thing that you're doing because they're also concerned about the company, maybe not to the degree you are. Primarily they're concerned about their jobs.

If they see that you're not doing your job, and you're doing things that could jeopardize the company, then it will rob them of their motivation to work for the company. You've just killed your culture.

Also, people on your team will be fuming mad if they feel they're not being treated fairly –at the same level as all their co-workers.

Keep Your Emotional Distance

You want to keep your emotional distance at all times. You can't become BFF with anyone in your company. You have to isolate yourself, *to some degree*, to really be an effective leader. Develop a professional bond with your team, have people like you and respect you, but nothing beyond that.

This can be a tall order. It's very tempting to get close to people, especially if you connect with them and like them. In an average working environment, people often make friends. Co-workers might date each other and so on. Social relationships are a big part of the day-to-day life in the workplace.

As a leader of your company, you have to find other places to network and develop relationships. There are lots of mastermind groups and networking groups for entrepreneurs, like EO Network, where you can do that. Your company is not the appropriate place to develop those types of relationships because the long-term consequences are absolutely devastating.

FREE BONUS VIDEOS

Want to discover breakthrough strategies on how to mitigate business risk *and* grow you're business faster than you ever imagined?

WARNING: This is like nothing you've seen before. These videos are a little weird.

After clicking the link below and opting in, you'll get immediate access to my series of Business Growth Acceleration videos.

http://profitswami.com/bookbonus

As you watch each video you'll discover unorthodox cutting-edge strategies, tactics, and tools that will allow you to smash through barriers holding your business back. Helping you achieve the success and recognition you deserve.

CHAPTER 9

Loose Lips Sink Ships

Loose lips can sink ships. I'm talking about confidentiality. For starters, it's very important that all your contractors (not just your employees or your business partners) **sign strict confidentiality and non-compete agreements.**

You have to go further than just having your team sign a confidentially agreement. Because they'll all but forget they signed it a month later. Take time to really talk about confidentiality with your team and explain why it's so important. They need to understand that *everything* that you do inside the company is confidential.

Mention it at monthly team meetings. Every time you make a breakthrough, remind your team that it's confidential. They shouldn't even divulge it to their spouse.

Some People Just Can't Keep a Secret

We had one guy in our organization who couldn't keep his mouth shut. He was a great guy. He was just a bit too generous when it came to helping our vendors and channel partners.

Whenever we made a breakthrough, inevitably one of our channel partners or vendors would suddenly find out about it. There were a couple of instances where we had to talk to him about it. In one instance, one of our vendors took the initiative on the advice this guy had given him.

Our servers were getting pulverized with denial-of-service attacks. It happened in late 2013, and it brought our company to a complete standstill. On top of bleeding $1000s a day in losses. Our technical team devised a way to protect against the DDoS attacks. After a while, it just stopped working. Like an army of blood-thirsty zombies, the DDoS attacks had eaten through our defenses.

I stumbled upon a DDoS protection service that showed a lot of promise. I had our technical team set it up. *All of our attacks went to zero, literally overnight.* The attackers actually escalated the attacks against us. Seeing that it wasn't working, they gave up after a week. ☺

DDoS attacks are a huge issue in our industry. Especially for the bigger players with more visibility. There's a good chance that many of our top competitors were attempting to fend off DDoS attacks themselves. For those reasons, I wanted the services we found kept a secret.

As you can probably guess, our one guy, who can never keep a secret, spilled the beans on our DDoS protection services to one of our vendors. And guess what? They immediately implemented it! As it turns out, they were also getting punished with non-stop DDoS attacks.

Normally, I wouldn't have cared, but this vendor also works with all of our top competitors. And it was in their interest to make sure our top competitors kept driving sales. Not cool. ☹

Keep Your Secrets Closely Guarded *Because You're Being Watched*

Like my team, you and your whole team are probably investing a ton of time on making breakthroughs in your company: figuring out ways to improve your sales process, figuring out ways to improve your business model and strategy, improving support and customer experience, etc.

Once you become a player in your industry, once you become a frontrunner, you are being watched like a hawk. *Your competitors will watch every single thing you do.* They setup services so they can get notified every time you make the tiniest change on any of your landing pages. Every change you make to your site is being analyzed and scrutinized.

They're buying your product. They're signing up for your services. They're doing everything to figure out what you're doing so they can rip you off and steal your business right out from under you.

The last thing that you need is an employee at a conference or on a conference call blurting out what they're doing. Over a bunch of drinks at a bar, when your staff is cutting up with vendors and competitors, they may start revealing your company's most closely guarded secrets.

I know for a fact that this happens all the time, because we ourselves have used this strategy successfully in the past. That is, **we had drinks with vendors and competitors in order to extract information from them!** We'd wait until they had a couple drinks in them, flatter them, and then start asking very pointed questions. Compliment them on their success. Praise them on their strategy. Pump up their ego like a hot air balloon. Then ask them how they figured it all out. ;)

If you're on the other side of the conversation and they're trying to butter you up for information then here's what you do: *be very vague and mislead them.* If they're a competitor and they're asking why your product is selling so well, say something like this, *"Oh yeah, once we got our new website up sales went up. That was a big key for us."*

I know, that might sound unethical. Misleading a competitor? Guess what, you're in the world of the sharks and the bears. You either ferociously protect your business or you'll be left for dead, with scavengers picking the meat off your carcass.

Your industry might be an open book where everyone shares their insider secrets and knowledge with everyone else. If that's the case then great, you can skip this whole chapter. However, for the rest of you: **protect your baby like your life depended on it.**

FREE BONUS VIDEOS

Want to discover breakthrough strategies on how to mitigate business risk *and* grow you're business faster than you ever imagined?

WARNING: This is like nothing you've seen before. These videos are a little weird.

After clicking the link below and opting in, you'll get immediate access to my series of Business Growth Acceleration videos.

http://profitswami.com/bookbonus

As you watch each video you'll discover unorthodox cutting-edge strategies, tactics, and tools that will allow you to smash through barriers holding your business back. Helping you achieve the success and recognition you deserve.

Playing to Win Versus Playing Not to Lose

In this entire book I've talked almost exclusively about how to mitigate risk.

Why?

Because launching a business is risky enough, once you launch you want to do everything you can to lower the risk moving forward.

However, you can go too far with this. You need to understand the difference between **playing to win** versus **playing not to lose**.

What exactly do I mean by that?

Listen, you can go too far with risk mitigation. If you get to the point of actively trying to avoid risk you're going to kill your company. You'll lose your entrepreneurial zeal and excitement that drove your company to success in the first place.

Avoiding risk is playing not to lose. If your focus is avoiding losing, avoiding failure, avoiding setbacks, then guess what? You'll never win.

Failure is a stepping stone to success. The faster you fail, in a controlled and manageable way, the faster you will succeed.

Risk hacking is about effectively managing risk, not avoiding it. You need to know what risks to avoid, which to mitigate, and which risks to *embrace*.

Making the Big Play

By protecting yourself against the 9 deadly traps I revealed in this book, you'll put your company in a strong position to make the big plays that will catapult your company to the next level. **These big plays are the risks you want to embrace.**

Maybe that big play is testing a new, huge advertising channel that could yield massive returns, but requires a $50,000 commitment to get it going.

Maybe that big play is opening an international branch of your company. Or maybe, launching a new product or service.

One of the big plays that I made at Boost was setting up a subsidiary in Poland. We had a full team of developers, designers, QA people, and even an office manager.

It cost us $50,000 to setup this entity, however, it was one of the smartest strategic decision I had made at the time. Not only were we able to build a team of developers in Poland at a fraction of the cost of a US team. They were rock stars. They rebuild our flagship product from scratch in 3 months time. And it was virtually bug free!

Now remember to apply risk hacking to each and every big play you're contemplating. You need to analyze each opportunity and look at the potential risk as well as the upside.

What's the worst that could happen if your big play doesn't pan out? You lose a bit of money and you're set back a month or 2? Or could it put you out of business?

If the upside is HUGE and the downside is a 1-3 month setback with a few dollars lost, then your decision is a no brainer. However, if you're going for an all or nothing play, where you risk losing everything, then you need to step back and rethink your strategy.

Remember: Play to Win!

FREE BUSINESS GROWTH ACCELERATION VIDEOS

Want to discover more strategies on how to mitigate business risk *and* grow you're business faster than you ever imagined?

WARNING: This is like nothing you've seen before. These videos are a little weird.

After clicking the link below and opting in, you'll get immediate access to my series of Business Growth Acceleration videos.

http://profitswami.com/bookbonus

As you watch each video you'll discover new strategies, tactics, and tools that will allow you to smash through barriers holding your business back. Helping you achieve the success and recognition you deserve.

About the Author

AMIT MEHTA

Amit Mehta is an author, speaker, blogger, and serial entrepreneur. As former Inc 5000 CEO, Amit built his last company to $11.6 million in revenue in just 3 short years.

Not only has Amit driven over $40 million in business through various different ventures in the last 10 years, he is also a recognized authority in business and marketing strategy. He has spoken over a dozen times at industry conferences and seminars, and helped countless individuals achieve success in their own businesses.

Amit began is journey as an entrepreneur in 2005. By 2007 Amit was making $2 million a year in revenue through his affiliate marketing business. From there he launched a blog called superaffiliatemindset.com. This blog soon became wildly popular, quickly establishing Amit as a reputed expert in the online marketing space.

In 2008 Amit helped create a training program that detailed his affiliate marketing strategy. This training program inspired and educated over 20,000 students and brought in over $6 million in revenue.

Amit co-founded Boost Software in 2010. He and his team struggled for 2.5 years to create and launch their flagship product. Once their flagship PC optimizer was launched, Amit took his company to 8-figures a year in revenue within 18 months.

Amit currently blogs @ profitswami.com

www.ingramcontent.com/pod-product-compliance
Lightning Source LLC
Chambersburg PA
CBHW072305200526
45168CB00014B/613